THE INNE

THE INNER TREES

Yvan Goll en 1928.

Selected Poems

YVAN GOLL

Edited by Thomas Rain Crowe

WHITE PINE PRESS/BUFFALO, NEW YORK

White Pine Press
P.O. Box 236
Buffalo, NY 14201
www.whitepine.org

Some of the material in this book first appeared in the following publica-tions: *House Organ, International Poetry Review, Asheville Poetry Review, Agulha: Revista de Cultura #53* (Brazil), *Beloit Poetry Journal, Nexus, Oxygen, Dimension 2, The Adiron-dack Review, Shearsman* (UK), *10,000 Dawns* (White Pine Press), *Dreamweed* (Black Lawrence Press), *10 Great Neglected Poets of the 20th Century* (APR), *Fruit From Saturn* (Sol Negro, *2013*, bilingual edition, Brazil),

"Jean Sans Terre Discovers the West Pole" translated by William Carlos Williams. From *The Collected Poems: Volume II, 1939–1962*, copyright ©1941 by William Carlos Williams. Reprinted by permission of New Directions Pub-lishing Corp.

Translations by WS Merwin, Robert Bly, Galway Kinnell, Paul Zweig, George Hitchcock, Frank Jones, Clark Mills, Kenneth Patchen, and Kenneth Rexroth are reprinted by permission of the translator or their heirs.

The translations from *Traumkraut/Dreamweed* reprinted by permission of Black Lawrence Press, *2012*.

Printed and bound in the United States of America.

ISBN 978-1-945680-25-0

Library of Congress number 2018947127

CONTENTS

From *10,000 Dawns* (1951)[7]

From *Dreamweed* (1951)[8]

PREFACE

Yvan Goll is one of the great lyric poets and authors of the twentieth century. He was born in 1891 in Alsace-Lorraine, which gave him a fluency in both French and German. He was active in both French and German pacifist circles during WWI and lived among other exiles in Zurich, Switzerland in 1917. In that year he also met Claire Studer, the woman who would become his wife and lifelong partner. His facility to absorb different cultures and points of view produced a large and varied body of work. As early as 1914 he was writing his epic poem "The Panama Canal" citing the toll to both humans and the environment in the building of that architectural marvel. Goll was in the avante-garde of various literary scenes from the beginning. A central figure in the world of Dada in Zurich and German Expressionism in Berlin alongside Hans Arp and Georg Grosz in the early twentieth century, Goll subsequently moved to Paris in 1919 with Claire, where they married in 1921. There, inspired by Apollinaire, he joined forces with Éulard as a founder of the French Surrealist movement. Yvan Goll's "Manifesto for Surrealism," included here and translated for the first time in English by Nan Watkins, appeared simultaneously, in October 1924, with André Breton's first Surrealism Manifesto. During Goll's life he published books of poetry illustrated by artists including Picasso, Léger, Dali, Braque, Chagall and Tanguy. An agent for Rhein Verlag, Goll brokered with Joyce the first German translation of *Ulysses*. As one of the French translators with Samuel Beckett, and in collaboration with Joyce, Goll worked to cast into French fragments from James

Joyce's last novel, *Finnegans Wake*.

As well as being a pre-eminent poet and translator, Goll was a playwright of enormous influence. His plays, such as "Methusalem" (1922), were the foundation upon which Ionesco built his "Theatre of the Absurd," and the launch pad for Artaud's "Theatre of Cruelty." Goll is generally considered to be the connecting link between Jarry and Ionesco. He is probably best known as a poet for his love poems and for his collections *Traumkraut* (Dreamweed) which was published posthumously in 1951 and *Le Chanson de Jean Sans Terre* (Landless John), published in New York in 1958 in translations by numerous American poets, including W.S. Merwin, Kenneth Rexroth, William Carlos Williams, Kenneth Patchen and Galway Kinnell. His *Manifesto of Realism*, in which he called for "a poetry of mystical realism," appeared in 1948.

Goll emigrated to the United States in 1939 at the time of the Nazi invasion of France during World War II, living at the center of the city's artistic life along with fellow émigrés Marc and Bella Chagall. In New York he became the celebrated editor of *Hemispheres* magazine through which he published the work of French and American poets —including Kenneth Rexroth, Henry Miller, William Carlos Williams, André Breton and Philip Lamantia —and several volumes of both his and Claire's poetry in English and French. During these years he befriended William Carlos Williams, James Laughlin of New Directions, and Kenneth and Miriam Patchen, among others, and spent several summers at the MacDowell Colony and at Yaddo, during which time he became an American citizen.

After the war, Yvan contracted leukemia and he and Claire returned to France in 1947. During his last weeks in the American Hospital in Neuilly outside of Paris, where he wrote the bulk of his opus *Traumkraut* (the first complete English translation, *Dreamweed*, being done by Nan Watkins and published by Black Lawrence Press in 2013), Goll quite literally survived on blood donated by fellow poets and artists. Upon finishing the text for the book that would ultimately secure his reputation as a poet in both Germany and France, Goll died on February 27, 1950 as the entry in *Who's Who in Twentieth Century Literature* says, "with a French heart, a German spirit, a Jewish blood and an American passport." He was buried in the Cimetière du Père-Lachaise in Paris next to the grave of Frederic Chopin.

Author of some fifty books of poetry, plays, fiction and essays, and recognized in Europe as one of the continent's greatest bi-lingual writers, Goll is arguably the most neglected poet of the twentieth century and is relatively unknown in the United States. The principal reason for his lack of fame in the U.S. and in English-speaking countries abroad is that very little of his work, until very recently, has been translated into English, and those translations were done in small-run limited editions. Among these are *Selected Poems* published by *Kayak* magazine and distributed by City Lights Books in 1968 with translations by the likes of Robert Bly, George Hitchcock and Paul Zweig; *Lackawanna Elegy*, translated by Galway Kinnell and published by Sumac Press in 1970; and Selected Poems translated by Rainer Schulte and Michael Bullock and published by Mundus Artium Press in 1981.

In his introduction to *Kayak's Selected Poems* Paul Zweig wrote: "Unlike the Surrealists, Goll loved a real woman, who was an unchanging presence in his life. He and his wife Claire formed a turbulent love-world of which he wrote continuously. And it may be that Goll will be remembered finally for these poems." (*Dix Milles Aubes*/*10,000 Dawns*—translated by Nan Watkins and myself and published by White Pine Press in 2004.) It is, perhaps, the eloquence, if not the prophetic suggestion of Zweig's endorsement, enjoined with the "simple visionary grace" of the poems themselves and Yvan Goll's importance to twentieth-century literature that have been the driving forces behind those who have translated his work. My selections here are in chronological sequence, citing many of Goll's most important poems written during the all-too-short arc of his life.

—Thomas Rain Crowe
January 2019

Surrealism Manifesto

Surréalisme

OCTOBRE 1924

1

IVAN GOLL

GUILLAUME APOLLINAIRE
MARCEL ARLAND
PIERRE ALBERT-BIROT
RENÉ CREVEL
JOSEPH DELTEIL
ROBERT DELAUNAY
PAUL DERMÉE
JEAN PAINLEVÉ
PIERRE REVERDY

jean michel place

Translator's Preface to Yvan Goll's Surrealism Manifesto

Though we associate the word "Surrealism" today with André Breton, whose "Manifeste du surréalisme" defined the word in October 1924, at that time it was not clear whose definition would prevail. Both Breton and Yvan Goll had used the term before 1920. Writing in 1919, Goll spoke of *Überrealismus* in his preface to his satirical German play *Methusalem:* "Thus the modern satirist must seek new stimulants. He has found them in surrealism and in the absurd." Breton has stated how he and Soupault also used the term *surréalisme* in 1919 to describe their automatic writing in *Les Champs magnétiques* (*Magnetic Fields*). Goll insisted that Apollinaire had been the first to use the term, calling his play published in 1917, *Les Mamelles de Tirésias,* a *"drame surréaliste."* The term surrealism began to appear in newspapers and literary journals in discussions of attempts to break with Tristan Tzara and the Dadaists, and by 1924 a line was drawn between Yvan Goll and his camp and Breton and his followers. Heated arguments ensued with many artists contributing to the debate.

In May 1924 Goll sponsored an evening of *"danses surréalistes"* bringing the German dancer Valeska Gert down from Berlin to the Comédie des Champs-Élysées. Breton and his friends disrupted the performance with cat calls and whistles, causing a general melee between the two groups until the police arrived to shut down the event. By the summer, articles and letters appeared in *Paris-Soir, Le Journal littéraire,* and other periodicals with Goll defending Apollinaire's views on heightened reality, while Breton insisted that surrealism was based on automatic writing to express the real process of thought. By August, Breton's group wrote that "surrealism is something quite different from the literary wave imagined by M. Goll" and they wanted "nothing to do with M. Goll or his friends either." Goll in turn criticized Breton for wanting "to monopolize a movement of literary and artistic renewal that dates well before his time and that in scope goes far beyond his fidgety little person." A blizzard of replies ensued until October, when both sides issued their own *"Manifeste du surréalisme."* Goll's two-page statement appeared in the single issue of his journal *Surréalisme,* while Breton's "Manifeste du Surréalisme," published by Simon Kra, took forty-four pages to define. Breton and friends eventually won the battle and went on to update their ideas by writing two further Surrealist Manifestos in 1930 and 1942.

Because Goll's "Surrealist Manifesto" has been lost to modern audiences, I offer it here to give a glimpse into another attempt to define one of the great artistic movements of the twentieth century. I find it especially relevant that though Goll composed his manifesto in French and was living in Paris at the time, his sensitivity to the German side of his personal Alsatian background and his cosmopolitan outlook were instrumental in creating his more global view of the term "surrealism."

—Nan Watkins

Surrealism Manifesto

October 1924

Reality is the basis of all great art. Without it there is no life, no substance. Reality is the ground under our feet and the sky over our head.

Everything the artist creates has its point of departure in nature. The Cubists, in the beginning, were well aware of this: as humble as the purist primitives, they bowed down before the simplest, most worthless object, and they went so far as to glue onto the picture a bit of colored paper, in its full reality.

This transposition of reality onto a higher (artistic) plane constitutes Surrealism.

Surrealism is a conception inspired by Guillaume Apollinaire. If we examine his poetic works, we find in them the same elements that were in the works of the first Cubists. The words of everyday life have for him "a strange magic," and it is with those, the primal matter of language, that he worked. Max Jacob relates that one day Apollinaire simply wrote down sentences and words that he had heard in the street, and from them he made a poem.

Solely with this elementary material he formed poetic images. Today the image is the criterion of good poetry. The speed of association between the first impression and the final expression determines the quality of the image.

The world's first poet declared: "The sky blue." Later another discovered: "Your eyes are blue like the sky." And much later one dared to say: "You have heaven in your eyes." A modern poet would exclaim: "Your heavenly eyes." The most beautiful images are those that bring together most directly and most quickly elements of reality that are far removed from each other.

Thus, the image became the favorite attribute of modern poetry. Up until the beginning of the twentieth century, it was the *ear* that determined the quality of a poem: rhythm, sonority, cadence, alliteration, rhyme: all for the ear. In the last twenty years the *eye* has taken its revenge. It is the century of film. More and more we communicate through visual signs. Today it is speed that determines quality.

Art is an emanation of life and the human organism. Surrealism, the expression of our age, takes into account the symptoms that characterize the age: it is direct, intense, and it rebuffs the arts that are propped up by abstract second-hand notions: logic, aesthetics, grammatical effects, wordplay.

Surrealism is not content to be the means of expression of any one group or one country: it will be international, it will absorb all the Isms that divide Europe, and it will take the vital elements from each.

Surrealism is a far-reaching movement of our age. It signifies health, and it will easily reject the tendencies to decay and morbidity that spring up wherever anything tries to establish itself.

The art of entertainment, ballet and the music-hall, the grotesque, the picturesque, art based on the exotic and erotic, the bizarre, the disquieting, the egoistic, frivolous and decadent art will soon cease to amuse a generation, which, after the war, needs to forget.

And this fake Surrealism, which some of the Ex-Dadaists have invented to continue to shock the public, will quickly disappear from the scene. They affirm the "absolute power of the dream," and make of Freud a new muse. It's true that Dr. Freud used dreams to cure mundane disorders. But to use that to justify the application of his doctrine to the world of poetry, isn't that confusing art and psychiatry?

Their "psychic mechanism based on the dream and the random play of thought," will never have the power to destroy our physical organism, which teaches us that reality is always right, that life is truer than thought.

Our Surrealism rediscovers nature, the primal human emotion, and strives, with the help of a completely new artistic medium, toward a structure, a purpose.

—Translated from the French
by Nan Watkins with Gerlinde M. Lindy

136 Columbia Heights
Brooklyn, N.Y.

15 Mars 1942

André Breton:

Si ce n'était que pour le chagrin d'une douce petite
fille, qui dut quitter une maison amie, parce que mon
nom fut prononcé,

~~J'aurais fait mes~~ ~~une ccuvent cette lettre,~~

Mais c'est aussi pour mettre fin au souvenir douloureux
de cette rixe à la Comédie des Champs-Elysées, que vous
avez évoqué hier soir.

Dois-je vous l'avouer? Ce coup de poing malheureux est
le seul, que j'aie jamais donné à un être humain, il est le
seul aussi, j'en suis sûr, que vous ayez jamais reçu dans
votre vie.

~~Dois-je vous avouer en même temps qu'il fut un geste~~
~~d'amour? J'ai frappé votre beau visage de Jochanaan, dans~~
~~Salomé parce que je n'aurais pas l'embrasser qu'ouvrir. Ce~~
~~fut un moyen suprême d'entrer en contact avec vous. J'en~~
~~ai souffert plus que vous, parce que c'est une chose~~
~~atroce pour vous.~~

A votre arrivée à New York, je suis venu vers vous
et vous ai tendu la main ~~cette main qui vous a frappé~~
~~jadis à la Comédie.~~ Le globe s'est tellement rétréci:
il n'y a plus que quelques rues, hélas, quelques chambres
qui s'offrent à nous. Nous serons obligés encore de nous
rencontrer: nous jetterons ~~le froid chez des amis, dans~~
~~le coeur de nos femmes.~~

~~━━━━━━━━━━━━━━━━━━━━━━━━━━━━━━━━━━━━━━~~

Ivan Goll

Il y a ici ce que je ne puis accepter et
ce que j'accepte. Je vous en donne acte
humainement, sans mépris. Il ne sera plus
jamais bruit de cette histoire: c'est malheureusement
tout ce que je puis faire, et vous rendre cette lettre.

André Breton

The Panama Canal

1914

The Work

I

Where once the Carib dreamily drove his light raft
Across oceans, where colorful parrots glided
In the overgrown jungle, and with fresh litanies
Pursued the monkeys, vicious and snarling, in swinging vines,

Where once the proud Spaniard, weapons glistening, kissed
The Earth in easy victory and like Adam already called it his own,
And likewise crushed the pagan god, who arose from the blazing fires,
Crushed it like a flower, for he followed a different path,

There small black railroads began to burrow,
Like worms after an August storm,
Into the broad breast of the mountain;
White signal flags of smoke fluttered.

The tracks ate gaping wounds into the chalky cliffs,
And all around rigid jungle palms were felled,
Split into logs, poles, stake—
Crane storks flew everywhere with long, poking necks.

II

But where stone piles lay, gray, flecked with green marl and bog,
The ground was as foul as rotting carcasses, and so greedy and used up
Was its feverish breath, that the dreams which it bore
Turned to toxic windrows, bared by a white sun.

All weariness the Earth sweated became a thick mosquito swarm,
Swelling slowly like smoke over graves and pasture;
The noonday sky grew hotter from their vermin and humming,
Each prick of sunlight they filled with a shot of poison.

And out of the swamps grew a pest with sickening green-brown
Eyes, vomiting across valley and plateau
And it had black teeth, and these stank so that when they bit,
Their victims already felt like carrion.

Yet why on earth did the brown oil wells
Spring up in Mexico's estates? One pest destroyed another!
Soon both ravine and jungle were soaking wet from the mottled grease,
And slowly in this wasteland there grew a grove of telegraph poles.

III

The rivers raged in summer, threw themselves foaming in their beds,
They swelled with power and roamed feasting through the valley;
But dams bent their course like a rapier of steel
And forced the waters to escape into steep concrete walls.
How they foamed! How they cried out!
Never to endure the false force of the dams!
And they built up and spewed forth, they plunged
Down the mountains of clay and filled them like sponges,

Tumbled again in old beds,
Quickly found the dry whirling rapids,
Choked down the newly-made houses and locks,
Sprang like dogs foaming with anger and frenzied barking.

Rats were in these shimmering waters causing
A shrill call into gap and crevice, over rails and dykes,
Their waves of tails gleamed like a game of knives,
And they stuffed themselves full on the bloated corpses of horses and men.

IV

All around, the Earth treed herself against the heinous crime,
And her thirsting, beefy body, turned tormented
Like a viper when it sheds its skin,
Until corrosive yellow sulfur spewed from smoky gorges.

Mountains, full of light and screams and running,
Fell like plaster and timber, clay avalanches
Buried men, rails and machines—
Dead silence piled up...

Not one sign had the earthquake given.
No hewer's axe fell, no stoker's lever shook,
But lizards' cracks had suddenly gnawed at the walls,
Roofs fell, floors burst, poles, rails, and rocks were shattered.

And a tired, tired rain flowed
And bemoaned the buried years of work.
Nowhere could a worker find his mate.
Where he had built new cradles, stretchers towered.

V

Meanwhile cities, cities had shot up like moss in the cliff's cracks:
Cites of brick, cities of straw or pointed tents.
Placed around a bathhouse, a hospital, a place of worship,
The workers' huts smoked, overflowing with sunlight, as in a daze.

All races mixed together: fiery and somber sons,
All gulped down the same raspberry ice, all braised fish from the sea
In the same pans, and they danced together on Sundays;
For just one thing bound them together: hunger and wages.

But not far from each city and each colony
Lay the great cities of the dead, colorful as gardens:
Daily, foreign folk melodies echoed there,
Daily, strange funeral processions of those with unshorn beards,

Others marched mute to the highest rite of the dead,
Still others wailed how they suffered at the sound of the gong.
Here the ever-alien earthly customs parted:
Where a cross stood with a wreath, where a stone lay raw and uncut.

VI

Gnawed by time, carved with blood, etched with gold beyond counting,
Through the lake, across cliffs and sandy desert
At last, the Canal.
Arc lamps led it by night from sea to sea.

But by day a sound of metal and steam and the hissing of a pump—
Sometimes just a dark cloud of dynamite hovered above —
And its reverberation and echo rebounded only distantly,
In the jungle, where no man yet walked.

At each entrance and exit the iron locks grew,
Each toll stamped by a petty hammer,
Monstrous flanks of incredible steel castings
Borne as by Prometheus deep into the bedrock.

And when these gates will open,
When the two hostile oceans kiss to cheers—
O then all peoples on Earth
Must weep.

VII (The Celebration)

Everything that is yours, Earth, will now call itself Brother,
All waters, the bitter and the sweet,
The cold streams and the springs, they rage,
Will flow together.

And there the heartbeat of Earth will always live,
Where the serpent of the Gulf Stream rings and encircles,
Sun-scaled and hot-blooded,
Around the capes and the islands of every zone.

Brazilian firewood, Northern pine trunks
And Europe's smooth, gleaming steel:
Ships from every dock and fjord turn up
Here at the Canal.

And the smoke of coal from foreign lands and latitudes,
From millennial forests, from deeply crushed quartz,
Grows like a broad tree up to the clouds, to the light,
Coming from the Black Earth.

So each patch of Earth pours forth its strength freely,
Becomes a Heaven over the peoples,
And from the roaring song of the motors and the seas
The Canal trembles.

Red, yellow, green pennants hang from the masts
Among garlands like birds in a giant cage.
They wave in a colorful parade in a flutter of foreign wind
From pole to pole.

Each man sings the anthem of his Lord and his country,
And there is a splash of languages and sounds;
But the savvy sailors and Argonauts
Understand each other well.

All the men in the harbor, on the docks, in the bars,
All talk to each other full of brotherly love.
Whether in pigtail, hat, cap, whether blond or brunette,
A man is a man.

Each man a brother quickly recognized,
This eye is mahogany, that a dagger of bronze,
This, like a star shining in quiet nights,
That, a flower wracked with pain.

Oh, the eyes of all drink to brotherhood
From the bottomless cup of universal love:
For here lies, welded as kin, all Earth's strength,
Here in the Canal.

Translation by Nan Watkins

Yvan Goll, Selbstporträt, 1949.

Jean Sans Terre

1936-1939

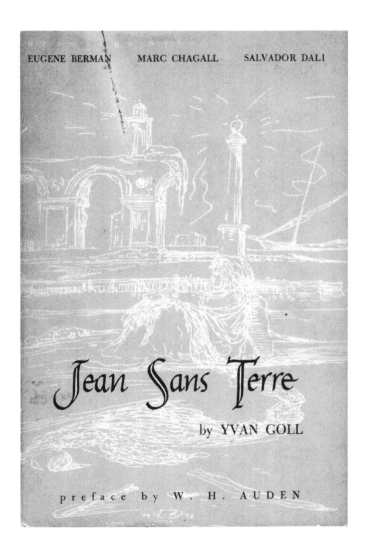

EUGENE BERMAN   MARC CHAGALL   SALVADOR DALI

Jean Sans Terre

by YVAN GOLL

preface by W. H. AUDEN

Jean Sans Terre Defined by Yvan Goll

Landless John is the man who removes his shoes
When he touches ground, better to feel it:
Its feminine sand and its angry rock
And the essence of its different clays

Landless John is the man whom you have met
At the Marché aux Poissons
Haggling over two sous for a kilo of dawn
Carrying trout like an armful of roses

Touching the beef and the pear near the heart
And the carp in his stillness
Feeling the material of things of the earth
Estimating the material of clouds

The arch-ancient man: all plays on words
All hands he shook are dead leaves
All the girls have kept his touch on their necks
Like a gust of almond-scented wind

In the morning his head bore the reed basket of sorrel
And at evening the tiara of seven wisdoms
His curls were wilder than David's
However his polished skull will roll on the boneyard

Landless John walks the roads leaving nowhere
He walks to escape his shadow which binds him to the soil
He wants to possess nothing on this earth. Will he
By singing, get free of his shadow, his other I?

—Translated by Galway Kinnell

Identity of Jean Sans Terre

Tantalus' son wrong from the start
In orchards of men I went unfed
Blank looks froze my flaming heart
The only loves I tasted fled

I walked the Street of Seven Sorrows
Went down the stairs the servants use
And passed the bridges of the Styx
The waiting rooms, the subterrainbows

I was the guest with a sad face
Innkeepers gave me a wide berth
My wine left bloodstains at my place
My shadows soiled the virgin earth

I slept among veronicas
Sucked eggs of nightingales at night
Butchered the magic unicorn
Ate birds but could not digest their flight

And landless still, after long forage:
Of the dead King I am not heir
The fruit on the Tree of Knowledge
Has spoiled; and I am hungrier

I will have been brief as the foam
On the crest of breakers afloat—
Born starless in the moonless gloom
My name but a catch in the throat

—Translated by Galway Kinnell

Jean Sans Terre Weds the Moon

Often Landless John
Drinks at night
The lunar beer
That foams light

Drinks drop by drop
The narcotic brew
Doubt also drinks
And anguish too

For the solitary
Shall always thirst
Yet never quenched
Who drinks love first

The pale liquor
Fills everywhere
Empty hearts
With a lost dream's flare

But too much splendour
Only veils
The thousand mysteries
Of starry angels

Stainless moon
Lotus of ether
Your snow of sand
Burns our flesh

Your amazon breast
Smooth, virginal
Makes men
Lovers of evil

With lewd love swelled
By Belphegor
Dogs of remorse
Your panther bore

You nourish the Nadir's
Somber, rude,
Vicious, man-
Destroying brood

But the nights when your face
Grows drawn and thin
Your pitcher breaks
Your milk turns green

The lovers' fervors
Disappear
All your magic
Turns to fear

You are no more
The fatal redhead
Your beer spumes
With venom tainted

Your golden palaces
Crumble down
The world of the shadows
Dies into dawn

—Translated by Yvan and Claire Goll

Jean Sans Terre on the Bridge

On the Pont au Change
John Landless turns
His strange face
To the burning water

After the adventure
Of the sevenfold tower
Is he seeking an omen
In the flowing waves?

The waters stride on forever
From the glaciers to the sea
And pass beneath the arches
Of the iron towns

Pass, inexhaustibly
Under the happy bridges
Of the cities of sand
Dancing in a round

John Landless bends down
From night and day
His white face
Over a dark love

What does he see coming down
Tirelessly
Over the fresh fields
Over the oceans?

Nothing but a cadaver
Nothing but a corpse
Seeking a harbour
After too much effort

And one of them comes up
To the divine bum
And slips in his pocket
Two cents for bread

John turns his head
Towards the good man
His heart stormy
His eye haggard and round

But the passersby go by
Over the dense thick river
And their dark mass
Drinks up the individual
John throws himself
Towards the parapet railing
But nothing beats more
In the turgid flux

Oh the sweet miracle
Has ended for ever
Over its tabernacle
Flows a green curtain

On the Pont au Change
John Landless turns
His strange face
To the knowing wind

—*Translated by Kenneth Rexroth*

John with No Moon

By the light of the moon
John who has no other
Meanders from one
City to another

Alone forever
Drunk with infinity
He wanders the world over
In exile eternally

Form linked with form
In pairs all except him
Sleep under the chloroform
Of a senseless dream

The moonlight shows
Courts and corridors
Golden windows
And platinum doors

Over the rooftiles
In the heart's core
The star spills
The oil of extreme languor

Oh even
The prison grills
Glow with crime
Like live coals

Only John keeps walking walking
With a mist wrapped around him
And finds nothing
But a bridge to shelter him

Always while he was young
His ambition was too great:
To grow drunk with tasting
Some pure absolute

Always vague, some height
Or arcane in his head
He even forgot
To make a bed

The sky all hung with lights
Turns like a fool
The radiant planets
Reveal jewel upon jewel
But John does not pause
To watch the cosmic lake
Head down he goes
His tired feet ache

Old all of a sudden
Chewing his spite
Poor John with no moon
Founders in the night

—Translated by W.S. Merwin

Jean Sans Terre the Assassin

John leaves the city of the Tantalids
Where human glances cast an evil spell
He takes the olive-tree in his valise
The secret of the king in his golden eyes

He saves the voice of the sunken fountain
And the unknown brother of his mirror
The nights of storm have not thundered in vain
Although his youth was throttled in a drawer

The forgers have burnished the dawn
The glaziers have refurnished the yesterdays
The world is still rich with Eleonores
His heart must break the record of the time

He steals the egg of the eagle and the phoenix
The grains of heaven and the stars of earth
But his flesh remains hungry without pride
He eats the bird without digesting the flight

He dances to the terror of the candles
He sings to the old silence of the mountains
His crown crashes to the potter's field
While his blue flower twines at the feet of the gallows

When he arrives at the Hotel with a cracked heart
He meets at last the queen of the chimera
At dawn he will kill her with a sneer
And leave his worn-out self at the checkroom

—Translated by Kenneth Patchen

Jean Sans Terre Purchases Manhattan

Manhattan Rock: phantom of vertical clay
Whose welcome greets the ship far off the coast
Before thy bankers and thy longshoremen
I lift my ancient hat a threadbare ghost

Kissed by the ocean thy inhuman Alp
Rises from those in sweat of labor drowned
Alp where the voiceless herds of sorrow graze
Where springs of soda gush from underground

And on the Hudson the red ferries wander
Like the swift shuttles driven by the weaver
Who weaves into his ancient tapestry
Figures that fade and melt into the river

But here old age like twilight comes more swiftly
Grass withers and the iron grows brown with stain
A hundred stories clothe the void
Solitude calls her sister but in vain

Close your accounts: boom years of the twenties
Drive from the Bowery all who are forgotten
Beneath the innocent giants of the earth
The graves of the rabbies lie rotten

The turnstile in the subway grinds the crowd
The paper pulp the pulp of destiny
The crowd that like a flood of sperm disperses
And scatters towards the beds of infamy

And at Times Square the merchants of the storm
Sell the split fifes and drums of death and offer
The candelabra of the festival
Insurance benefits for those who suffer

Take out a mortgage against human wisdom
Lease the suburban greensward in the Park
The Fates in combine purchase shares of cotton
The stock-exchange of irony is closed and dark

If man climbs to the peak of Jacob's ladder
And smiles down from the hundred-second story
He stumbles down the staircase of old age
Towards Job's poor bone-yard far from fame and glory

Sell death buy the Eumenides
Sell wind sell liberty
Buy dream sell the Hebrides
Oh sell and buy and sell and sell and buy
I buy Manhattan for a single smile
I sell it back for immortality
Some day this white sand will no longer glisten
The rock will dream of a forgotten city

—*Translated by Clark Mills*

Jean Sans Terre Discovers the West Pole

John Landless leads his landless folk
All those who owned no window and no door
And nothing but the bed to die and to be born
And the shadowy bitch licking their misery

They wander on the roads of centuries
Riding the meager mare of hope
Seething with the yellow fever of the night
Feeding on black milk and bitter herbs

They leave the upright house in the godless street
Stores of oblivion factories of ghosts
They even leave the blooming tree of knowledge
On which are hung their brothers and their fears

Although they know the codes of human reasons
And touch the antic oxen at their tail
And grasp the trout at the garnet ear
And value fur and pulp and fat

They go ahead harassed by the tempest's fury
By glowing snow and by the wind of myth
Chased by the trumpets of the Scythian wrath
And by the blizzard of sharp whetted eyes

John Landlesss led them out of time and doubt
Out of the iron cities and the Pharaoh towers
Out of the depths and oblique corridors
Along the heedless roads

A gray-haired angel took them to the hill
Offering them the conquest of the Western Pole
The moon-bird flew and dropped his golden feathers
Over the dust of waking centuries

Here the landless folk will build Westopolis
Again stores of oblivion factories of ghosts
Again the upright houses down the godless street
And trees of knowledge where friends are hanged

John Landless flees at dawn back toward East alone.

—*Translated by William Carlos Williams*

Jean Sans Terre at the Final Port

To Claire Sans Lune

John Landless sailing on a helmless boat
Through waveless oceans towards shoreless sands
Lands on a dawnless day at a townless port
Knocks at a houseless door with his boneless hands

Yet he remembers well these ancient galleys
These ageless slaves these steamless steamers
These barless streets these gazeless windows
These sleepless walls these godless dreamers

He knows this woman without faith and face
Who combs the curls of her fallen hair
He knows her restless bed her fireless embrace
Her love without desire and despair

He wonders why the cranes don't stop to load
Why they load caskets and the newborn grain
The wrathless lemons and the joyless wines
Why they load coal and unload ash again

This leather never will be shoe
This cotton never bandage the soldiers
This lumber will not heat the homeless
This wheat never feed the paupers

But who is he this nameless passenger
Who was not born and has no right to die
No reason to embark or disembark
But who is he this passenger without a lie?

—Translated by William Carlos Williams

44

Fruit From Saturn

1946

ATOM ELEGY

To Lukas Foss

II.

The ray of rays shatters my insane soul
And feeds me with inhuman energy

O new nativity in the protean cradle
O death festival for the old sore thighs of earth
Unlocking the concentric love

The Tree of Science saturn-blossoming
Enhances the real trinity

Spiritual rose from aged centuries
The master wheel among the world of wheels
This rose was light
This rose was round
As is the rose of universe
As is my eye in which all eyes are hidden
Round as the dew
Round as my head
In which the stars of a million atoms ripen

III.

In the beginning was the word
In the beginning was the number

The word: prime essence out of which
Through seven thousand nights of labor
The Kabbalist compounded seventy names of God

The word: the Guide to the Perplexed
Out of the coal of memory

The element of elements
Poured in the mental furnace

O to the music of the withering stars
To the delirium of pregnant gongs
Out of my algebraic dreams
And old old fears
Dance: my beloved atom
Transfigured carnotite

IV.

The Divine Garment clothed my blandished thighs
Against the holy beasts and the mad angels

And the 10 numbers sprang from Adam's forehead
The spheric fruit of the Sephiroth
Became the emblems of his crown

The cipher: birthplace of the sphinx
Memorial of prenatal dawns

Past Delphi's tripod and cathedral domes
Pythagoras' revolving harmonies
Past Bruno's pyre and Einstein's time

Riding the wheel
The 10 again in sweet uranium 235
The seven-colored ray
Bursting from dying Self
The Infinite raped in Alamogordo

The Myth of the Pierced Rock

1947

**THE MYTH OF THE
PIERCED ROCK**

Yvan Goll

Translated by Frank Jones

Pérce Rock is an isolated mass of Devonian limestone, in Canada, on the Gáspe coast, opposite the village of Percé. The Indian name Gaspé means End of the World.

The cliffs of the rock are smooth and so sheer that a local law forbids any attempt to climb them. At high tide the rock is transformed into a wave-beaten isle. At low tide one can walk around it dry-shod. The ocean constantly gnaws at the stone and has bored into it a kind of gate, twenty meters high, through which boats can pass. Hence its name: Pierced Rock.

The entire mass consists of a conglomerate of gleaming yellow and reddish iron, veined with limestone. The rock is said to contain forty-four kinds of fossils. Its summit is inhabited by thousands of birds, which give the stone an air of extraordinary life.

The theme of the poem is the life and death of a rock, its somber, seemingly sterile exile in the sea which hatches life in the eternal circus of wedding, its dance among precious stones, its yearning song of alluring dawns, and finally its liberation and disintegration in the atomic age.

—Y.G.

II.

Living Rock
The Navigators recognized you
Chimera of the North
Changing by angle by eye by hour

> From the front Eagle
> From the side Lioness
> From the air Snake

Rock more restless than the living
More spiteful than the sea
Crazier than your birds

Does the lava-feathered Eagle await the end of suns to fly away?
The Lioness still digests the herds of caribou surprised in the gneiss clearing
The Snake whose gang is oblivion escapes in vain from chthonic night

> Waiting of the creature
> Patience of the future

III.

Precious Rock
More delicate than the flower of the lightning tree
More restless than the gill of the shark

Sinuous torso
Leaning over your mica breasts
I saw I saw
Heart's amber light you up
I touched your jasper flesh juicier than elk meat
Plucked the petals of your quartz daisies
And took your radioactive agate hand in mine

Under their gypsum lids
Your staring eyes heft two interior lakes
Your blood has started circulating
Rich with the hemoglobin of Cambrian dawns

In your turquoises of loveliest water
The tenderness of stones has revealed itself

XIV.

Treasure Rock
Open yourself
Open your chalk hands
Your anhydrite forehead
Open your dikes and your quicklime flanks

Weak ultramontane masonry
Yield to my plummet yield to my eye
yield to my little finger which divines the Essence

To go down down
Into your petroleum lungs
Into your barium spleen where dwells the laughter of the gods
I must find the carnotite road
As far as the naphtha biles
As far as the oxidized hysterias
Putting my ear to your petrified conch
I hear the collapse of your churches
I watch the smelting of leads the despair of dolomites
The fossil sand dollar points to noon.

XV.

Atom Rock
Does the fossil sand dollar point to midnight?
Gulf Stream and Japan Current loosen their grasp of madrepores
The matrices of the universe slow down

The eagle's spiral narrows the lioness' eye contracts
The snake is metamorphosed
Gold crumbles on temples
Blood dries on armorial bearings

The rock Heart begins to beat
Fruit more male than the lemon more female than the mango
Ripens in pitchblende orchards
The atom fraternizes with exhausted Saturn

Oh wedding of weddings
Microbial numbers invade the rock flesh
An equinoctial leaven raises the stone bread
And a yellow uranium joy
Fills the earth long dead of patience
Virgin chained amid broodings of migrations
More learned than Sodom's pillar of salt
Farther-sighted than the Sphinx's frightened eye
Explode!
Pierced rock! Split rock!
In your atom heart!

Ivan et Claire Goll avec Marc, Bella et Ida Chagall, Bois-de-Cise, 1924

Lackawanna Elegy

1947

Lackawanna Elegy

America
     The tongues of your rivers burn with thirst
America
     The coal in your mountains goes mad with sunlight
America
     The arms of your sequoias ask pity of the storms
America   America

     Your heart's drum
     Eats its own bones
     The eyes of your clocks
     Turn counter-clockwise seeing the past

And on her crumbling headland the Indian woman
Turns toward you eyes weighed down with asphalt
Her mercury and orange head shrinks just slightly
Her small breasts bared to the gnawing white ants

     She paints on the sand
     The oracle which a night effaces
     A rattlesnake gripped in her teeth
     She exorcises the white ghost
     Locked in his Kiva of hate

A shiver of feathers down the reed of the spine
Stirs your ash body America
A thorn is stuck in your twilight brow
A thorn is sown in the fields of hemp
A thorn is screwed into the heel of your dancers

America beware of your past
Of the Katchinas filled with menace
For wrath ripens its fiery apple

In the orchards of the Appalachians
In the desert colored by witches

In the rose-garden of your sick soul
The holocaust waits to begin.

Show Boat

America skull filled with ants and red comets
America who spellbinds me who lives in me
Your cities rotting on the dunes of memory

Stop! Stop! At the boomerangs of your highways
Stop! At the totems of your gaspumps
Whose ether and tar eyes
Open and shut under the anisette moon

Stop! I tell you! the future rides on your back
And the Indian's sacrificial gaze
Makes the jazz platters spin backward
Wheels of dollars gold sunflowers

Stop! Stop! America! America!
Show on the showboat's burning boards
To the beaches sparkling with pink and blue eggs
The pain of old man River
A shot of nostalgia rattling his green eyes
At each crossroad of water.

Bridges

I have passed my life on bridges
Between the two shores
Of truth and lie
Of presence and desire
The right and the left
Always in love with each other

I have passed over the Pont Neuf in Paris
The Ponte Vecchio in Florence
The Danube Bridge between snow and rain
Washington Bridge between reason and madness
The Bridge of Sighs
The Bridge of the Dead

Always straddling emptiness and danger
Time's witness
Plucking apart the sea-green compass-flower
Wave by wave
Petal by petal

And as I leaned out from the parapet
Filled with thirst and sleepy
My gaze struck the lead mirror
My Gorgon face capsized
My snake hair.

Lackawanna Mannahatta

Lackawanna Mannahatta
City submerged under a sea of stars
Gnomes of ball-bearinged motors drowse in beds of mint

Daybreak has found
Truth lying murdered in a thicket of thorns
The red shock of his hair
One day will lead the revolt

An unclean blood pulses through the city's cables
The bricks of our temples are made of the menstrual flow
From an army of one-breasted Amazons

Evil takes on vegetable shapes
Caterpillars in their tawny fur
Ruin pastoral Pæstums

In a suburb of Lackawanna
I will come back on fishmarket day
Some meatless Friday
When the fishwives smell of the tide coming in under their triple skirts.

Wings of Water

Lackawanna! The boatmen sing
Lackawanna on the days of waiting
Lackawanna on the pregnant nights

And the cruel birds appear over the futile waters
The sun's crutches   The water's wings
In a flight more fatal than an ellipse

Lackawanna! The dying sing
Lackawanna on empty hearts
Lackawanna on dry lips

From innocent clouds the guilty birds wheel down
Weaving their crown of hunger
On corpses that were expecting light

Lackawanna! The boatmen sing
Lackawanna on the days of waiting
Lackawanna on the pregnant nights.

Fish of Wandering

After the storm I haggle
Over the fish of wandering and heartbreak
With my finger I twirl the red disk of the ear
And make the sweet milt spring up

I buy a dead fish to lengthen my life
I fry it in the oil of noon and knowledge
I crown it with the laurels of genius
And I eat it leaf by leaf plucking it like a periwinkle

But do not ask its mouth shaped by pain
Why its green lip remains bitter
Why the gold wave collapses
Why pure water shrinks from the earth.

Brooklyn Waterfront

The waves shuffle the cards and hide the secrets of life
In the twilight foundries they make counterfeit money
Worthless after five minutes

A woman out there becomes a flawless black dancer
Whom I would have loved, whom I would have loved
If the great western ibis were not already bearing her away
Bloodied by the rosebed at the statue's foot

All this enters my soul mixes with my blood
Glares back from my eyeball
Angry sun setting in the heart of a ghost
Harder to grasp than Ganymede's cloud

Shall I see you ever again? Shall I see you tomorrow?
With what new wounds in my neck? With how many
Fewer songs in my throat?

O bluefish of jade whom I did not fry!
O dauphins of God who have dumped me here
On a dock that feeds unearthly smells to the wind
Beside warehouses where dwarf families live
Their methods of farming the darkness produce a strange philosophy
Their gods are products of fear
They live in the cellars of the darkness, these blind
Dwarfs who have lost even the organ of seeing!

Balconies Suspended Over Lackawanna

O Bagdad Palaces, O shacks of Damascus
I remember your balconies suspended over Lackawanna
Your lamps flashing and going out night after night
And your fishmarkets closing before noon

I see your Pharaohs climb the balustrades
And lose an army by opening an eye
And soon their corpses horribly alone
Bob in the slimey river at the drinking hour

Old names come back in coughs of the wind
Unfinished loves call to each other among the reeds
But the dogs from customs make their shady rounds
Those we thought faithful will come and scrape our bones.

Lackawanna Elegy

Hypnotized we watch the river go by
We lean out
Our shadow wavers far down the depths
Hesitant to know the truth

Which is everything the river hides
With his feverish hands of waves
Guiltily as a thief
In his pockets full of vice and darkness

Just as we hide the shadows of our days
In locked chests
And throw the key without making a copy
Into the swirl of daily streets

Then placed on the riverbank
In widows' weeds and shirts of gloom
We find ourselves standing lost in thought
Watching our last hopes flow out

The wreckage of our own house we watch floating past
We let the small hands of our daughters sink under
Gazing clear and steady we no longer hear
The cries of submerged nations.

10,000 Dawns

1951

CLAIRE ET YVAN GOLL

DIX MILLE AUBES

illustré par

MARC CHAGALL

#

Your hair sets fire to the largest burning light of the century.
Your brow is the blackboard on which the secrets of men are scrawled.
Your eyes are two diamonds glued into the face of the Sphinx.
Your neck is an Eiffel Tower painted in pink.
Your lips are twin boats that dance on the Red Sea.
Your teeth are lined up like the keys of my piano.
When you speak, the acacias bloom.
Ten creeks laugh.
And when you walk,
Everything swings!

#

Of all the trees in the forest, in the orchards, and in the fields
Of famous ancestral baobab trees with wooly beards
Of ancient imperial oak trees that are the palace of eagles
Of almond-trees in pink hats
Of incestuous lemon trees smitten with their blossom and their fruit
Of weeping willows that weep again on tragic lakes
Of chivalrous palms with a soft heart under their breastplates
Of fir trees that give us back the senile snow
Of rickety old lime trees in the courtyards of the poor
And of ascetic cypress with the oeuvre of snakes

Of all the trees in the forest, in the orchards, and in the fields
I prefer the smoking tree with ebony leaves
Whose ephemeral vision we plant in the evening
On our neighbor's roof
The tree that rises and climbs with us into orbit
And, from above, throws back to us the magic fruit of our dreams.

#

I want to be that birch tree
That you so love.
I would have 100 strong arms to protect you,
100,000 green and gentle hands
To caress you!
I would have the best birds in the world
To wake you up at dawn
And console you at night.
I would pour you from the petals of the sun
In summertime.
I would wrap your fearful dreams in my shadow...
I want to be that birch tree
Who carves out your grave
With its roots
In order to embrace you again and again

\#

Your eyes are everywhere: on the ripe fruit
In the tree of Knowledge

Your x-ray eyes see more
Than those of the blind Sphinx

Your bitter almond eyes
With the carnal heart of an apricot

Your storybook eyes
Stolen from the goats of Tibet

Your eyes under each eyelid
In every rose in France

Your eyes in the feathers of peacocks
In the scales of carp

Your round green wheels
On the road to catastrophes

Your eyes of gin
That I drink from to the point of madness

Your starry eyes
Which make up the constellation of Perseus

Your mediterranean eyes
In whose deep ground I am buried, and laugh.

#

I have grown old waiting for
Wet Februaries and tardy Aprils
To offer you a sprig of lily of the valley.
I have sat up countless pale nights
Conferring with the moon
About your faithfulness.
I have held up telegraph lines all summer
Waiting for your blue call.
And through nights of crying
I caressed the handwriting of your letters.

Any season is good for the work of the heart:
Farmer of the sky,
I sow and I reap the stars,
To feed us, and feed us well, my love!

\#

In 100 years the fountains will rain on you again.
The crows will wear veils forever,
And the nightwind will sell your sigh
Until someone calls it death!
But nothing will smoke more than your soul
That intoxicates the waking spring,
Where you are a shamrock
Or a begonia.
And strawberries taste like your lips
Where your death-proof love
Is muse for the Mother Earth.

\#

I wear you like a tattoo
Your smile on my eyelids

On my lips is etched
Each of your kisses

The acid of your tears
Is burning my shirt collars

And your letters that will last forever
Have filled up my suits

Tattooed
Against all their advances

Why do you even care
That other women would want to sell me love!

\#

This is the season of jealousy:
My eyes drop like leaves
From the fall of my life.

Rain strokes my hair
With widowed hands.
Sister Sorrow, sitting on the boot of my car,
Cry for me!

Iron and lead
Are not as heavy
As love.

\#

O, I want to complain
About the owl who knocks on the doors of night,
Always dressed in autumn,
Fed on moldy old stars
And bound to thousand-year-old trees . . .
I want to complain
About the smart owl
Who fakes eternal pain
While making love,
Or cries like the root of all evil.
Who with a million wounds
Pours out all his white blood . . .

In the cold night
You listen to my complaints.
But can't you hear my heart near you
Beating to the drum of death!

#

We will always be alone
Wrapped up in each other's skin
Like two shrouds!

Mouth to mouth
Like two balconies
We throw ourselves the red flowers of love.

With our hands clenched in a fist
Believing to bond the forces of flesh
Like cement to blood.

Useless! Useless!
Useless smiles house-painting our heads!
Useless tears that stick to nothing!

In the desperate embrace
Between the two of us entwined
Stands our shocking solitude.

\#

You are elusive.
Like a brook
Gliding through mint bushes!
Sometimes you shiver
To the music of my metaphors
When I bend over you.
The stars light up
When you look at me.
You belong to me
As the eye belongs to the face.
And with one of my songs
On your lips
You will rendezvous with death...
But you escape me, you fly off
Like a chord from my mandolin.
Elusive.
My love, my life!

#

10,000 dawns my angel, 10,000 dawns.
10,000 times the eye of the sun
Has come to open again our eyelids.

10,000 dawns for this one night
Of our love.
Your head sculpted in my arms.
The rose garden of your hair
On fire with 10,000 red roses.

O what fireworks! And the 10,000 voices of waves —
How many moons have passed
Delirious or sad
Covering us with the ecstasy of snow.

And of old men who have lent us their eyes.
And of children who have eaten our hearts
In the 10,000 dreams of love.

10,000 dawns, my angel, 10,000 dawns.
10,000 eggs filled with
Birds and their songs.
10,000 sunyolks
More than make up for this death
Of 100,000 stars.

Dreamweed

1951

I. GOLL

TRAUMKRAUT

LIMES VERLAG

Alasam

Alasam
The unshed tear
In the hollow of my skull

From this there grew
Long long generations later
A dreamweed
Night-yellow murder-sallow

Unique flower
Unnoticed by the bees

This Holy Body

This shaky house of bones
Built upon sand
Lodging for my ancestors

From my eyes they follow
All the roads I take
My spleen is their kitchen
Where they cook with fat and blood

In the niche of the ruins my mother still sleeps
Old men's tobacco smoke clings to her larynx

My holy body!
Sacrificial animals roar deep within me
And beef loins exhale their stench every Saturday

My mouth still houses
Century-old magic
In my ears I hear a ringing and a singing
And no God

Rosedom

Moon-rose
That burns in the heads of beasts
Brain-rose
Skinned from skulls
O hot-tempered rosedom

As long as the wheel of the rose
Turns and turns
The noonday rosary
Raves in fevered fields
And the rose-eye bores
Into my waking sleep

Yet woe if the Unrose
Ascends from the metals
And my rose-hand rises
Against the sun-rose
And the sand-rose withers

O rose rose of roses
That alone blazes for the roseless

Job

III.

Last olive tree, you say?
Yet golden oil
Drips from my branches
That learned how to bless

In the glass house of my eyes
The tropical sun grows hot

My root-foot is rammed in marble

Hear O Israel
I am the ten-bread tree
I am the book of fire
With the burning letters

I am the three-armed chandelier
Occupied by knowing birds
With their seven-colored gaze

South

The South Wind rattles in my vertebrae
A door in my chest bursts open
But of all the doors which one is it?
Tell me which it is so I can flee from myself

South brotherly South
Brush the question from my brow
Thaw this loner free
From the grieving glaciers

In Fields of Camphor

You are at home in fields of camphor
In iodine swamps you drink yourself finally young
The brown brandy of roots
Nourishes you better than jugs of sun

A torch blazes and reels in the oil of your eyes
A fire makes music with flute and drum
Your ancestors' skeleton dances at the festival of decay

The noble yellow flower
That blooms once every thousand years
Slowly uncoils from your ribcage

The Sun Cantata

The many-armed god dances for us
The fire-haired chieftain ponders and sings
    Light-drum and sea-harp resound
    To greet Him the Wondrous One

From which tree of fire did you fall
O fruit that consumes its own seed
    That still burning of phosphorous
    I take in my unwitting hands

The nut in whose shell the primal mind lives
The naked nut beguiled by its own pleasure
    Begets itself over and over
    In the crazed law of self-adoration

Yet unborn suns of coalmines
And already consumed suns of evening smoke
    I bind in bouquets of blue suns
    For your incessant blind nights

The cogwheel of impatience saws away the noon
The sunflower grows weary in its standing sleep
    Almonds fall from our eyes
    Peaches plunge like meteors

O Sun! Be cruel with your seed!
Lay your death eggs in our ear!
    So that from each cranial crack
    The flower of madness blooms copper!

In the sun's head amber time grows old
Time that loses itself in thought and forgets! Time
    Of the plunging brook and the putrid pond
    Of falling moons in blind skies

Ice-bird time in the sun's memory! Sing
Of the uncherished springtimes: Sing of the heart
    Which buried alive for millennia
    Calls you from the rubies in the mountain!

To Claire-Liliana

Beloved, you are my river
On your right bank is the past
On your left bank is the future
Streaming together we sing the present

The decaying trees, they gaze after us
The birds of deliverance, they fly before us

In your right eye I am a diamond
In my left eye you are velvet

The sun revolves from your right shoulder
The moon wanes in my left hand
Beloved, I am your river
Flowing together we are silent in the present

                                                                                      &

Eavesdropping on your sleep
I hear the blind pianist
Playing on your ribs
I hear the black waves of night
Breaking on your tender breastwork
The brute angst stomping through your bushes
And bridges bursting over your bloodstream
Eavesdropping on your sleep
I count the pulse of my days

&

How many morning suns have seen
Their image reflected in our eyes!
And the shaping of the day was at our discretion

The dew owed its existence
To the pure invention of love

Even where typhoons grew fat on jungle beasts
And threw their long yellow wings
Around unstable islands

Even there our living monument to love stood firm
Your smile, my beloved,
Solved the darkest riddles of all

&

I hear the freezing bird of morning take flight from you,
The raucous one, from the benevolent ovens of sleep
                    Beloved, my fire!

I hear the dark language of noon tumble out of you,
The stern, mature garnet of long wise tolerance
                    Earth, my beloved!

I hear the golden ram's horn of evening call in you,
The deeply buried fear of an uncertain end,
                    My beloved, the air!

I hear the old seas of midnight rush through you
And the menacing magic of never-wearying breath,
                    Water, my beloved

To Claire

Written in the Hospice
December 1949 to January 1950

Did I pluck you in the gardens of Ephesus
The curly hair of your carnations
The evening bouquet of your hands?

Did I fish for you in the lakes of dream?
An angler on your meadows' shores
I threw you my heart for food

Did I find you in the dryness of the desert?
You were my last tree
You were the last fruit of my soul

Now I am wrapped in your sleep
Bedded deep in your repose
Like the almond in its night-brown shell

&

The rumor is spreading
That your feet become a fish tail
When you dive to fetch me fruit from the sea

The children are already whispering
That your arms are willow branches
That catch the clouds
Where you bed me down

It is no longer a secret
That your lips bleed
To save me from snowy hunger
In my nights of dying

Soon everyone will know
That your body has been hollowed
A fragrant grave
For our twin death

The Fear Dancer

The fear in your hands is light as smoke over fields
You are caught in a tower of thorns
You glide through its walls yet you never find your way to me

The fear in your hair is yellow as the glow of dying candles
The fear in your voice is inscrutable as fog
You hurl yourself against my chest and yet I cannot feel you

You are a fear dancer disguised as autumn crocus
In a circle of red warriors you are buoyed by the music of bones
Yet you never break the circle and you never glide to me

What is whispering in your head? Whom do you call your tormentor?
Never has the reddish-green of your eyes smoldered so deceitfully
As in your dealings with the weapon-glistening foe

Fear is the burning wool dress—the blue one that I bought for you
It embraces you and keeps you from coming to me
You are burning in its fabric and crying like a wailing bird

The Rain Palace

I have built you a rain palace
Of alabaster columns and rock crystal
     So you can transform yourself for me
     Ever more beautiful in a thousand mirrors

The water palm nourishes us with its gray grog
We drink silver wine from tall pitchers
     What mother-of-pearl drumming!
     Drunken dragonfly in the rain forest!

In your liana cage of vines you long for me
Magic bees suck the rain-blood
     From your blue-eyed goblets
     Singing herons stand guard

From rain-windows we watch how time
Drifts with rain-banners across the sea
     And with battle troops of foreign storms
     Ends miserably in ancient swamps

I dress you in rain-diamonds
Disguised Maharaja of the Realm of Rain
     Whose worth and laws are weighed
     In hallowed years of rain

But on the sly in the Hall of Pearls you knit me
A rain-shawl from hemp and tears
     Wide enough for us both
     A warm and everlasting shroud

Yvan & Claire Goll with Carson McCullers and Maurice Speiser
at Yaddo in upstate New York, 1946

YVAN GOLL: Selected Poems

1968

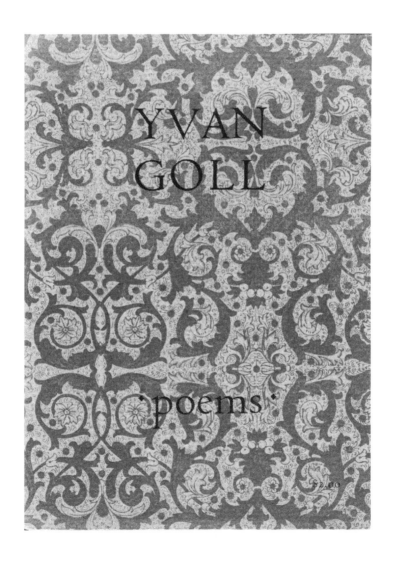

Chagall

Ode to Autumn

Why are the elms already
Tearing up their clothes
And throwing their arms around
In insane fear?
The golden calm of summer
Has left them.
The lions are lost
In the gray grass,
The dandelions of happiness,
The promises of lovers,
Already forgotten,
Die away in the underworld.

The great king
The knower of strange things
Lord of the woods
Gives up his fight
Against clouds,
He lets the rusty sceptre
Hit the ground,
The apple of wisdom
And all the jewels
Of the crown rot.

In the rustling
Honeysuckle of the marshes
The chest of the terrified marten thumps.
The dragonfly breaks
In two above the pond
Like delicate glass.

Only the centaurs
With red beards
Run down
The hill joyfully,
Hoofs throwing sparks,
And their sparks
Glimmer in the moss.

The leaves get free
From their branches
Like swaying and wounded hands:
Underneath they build
Up a coppery tomb
For the birds that are dying.

In the ruins
Of the bird castle
The night owl still lives,
Lighting up the future
With his huge eyes.

—Translated from the German by Robert Bly

The Inner Trees

The drunken trees
The trees of my life drunk with death and hot
Are leaping up out of my head
Full of fruit, using roots
Hands and suns
Nimble and thoughtful animals

Saturn's light is burning
In the eye of the golden frog
All the time the comets
Blossom in the pastures

—Translated from the German by Robert Bly

The Hut of Cinders

We hadn't a house like the others safe under the mountainside
We had to wander ever further
Through snow that was neither salt nor sugar
Past the round tenpins of the moon

You called to your guardian birds
Which high in the stratosphere flew to African graves
The road of forgetfulness turned in great loops
And no pale flower pondered on the path

Toward midnight we found a hut of cinders
The laughing howls of wolves could be heard
I held them off with torches
And in the creek thick with nettles
I caught an oilfish
For a long time it kept us warm
The bed we carved from snow was broad

And then the miracle occurred:
Your golden body shone like a nocturnal sun

—*Translated fro,m the German by George Hitchcock*

I Loved You in Every Blackbird

In every blackbird
I loved you
In every gust of wind
I felt your presence

We stood at the edge of the glacier
Heart to heart
In the sagebrush we startled the scorpion
Hand in hand

From the spires of Strasbourg
We sang a song in the evening
Mouth to mouth

Alas, on the lonely path to sleep
I stumbled
And drowned

—Translated from the German by George Hitchcock

Do Not Call Death

Do not call death!
Do not wait for the black earth
To chisel our faces.
Eternity is only
In your springing laughter.
I do not believe in the silence of stones;
I believe in the nightingales that repeat your voice,
In the antelopes that copy your walk;
The sunflowers, those clocks of love,
Mark only the happy hours.
And that one dusk
Where the gods themselves grew jealous
Of a kiss made with honey and electricity,
Is worth more than the century of centuries.

—Translated from the French by Paul Zweig

Why Should the Summer Come Back

Let it be November on the earth
Because you are so sad
Let the sick moon die
And the night with its plaintive trees
Tear the curtain of the sky—
I need dogs with voices that are moaning
I need walls moistened with rain, that tremble
Where the shadows themselves are afraid.

For it would be terrible to think
That somewhere soft roses are flowering
That streams as wild as children
Leap over the moss-covered slopes
That swallows are cheerful
That stars are still shining
When the smile has left your face

—*Translated from the French by Paul Zweig*

Blood Rose

All the trees of winter
Had already forgotten their names and their birds,
Waiting like beggars in the forest

And a bush stood straight in the wind
Poorer, more thin than all the rest
Its arms were more like bones

But when I came near
To caress one of its branches
Suddenly it bled

And in this great red drop
Round roses were formed
That is how saints and lovers bleed

—Translated from the French by Paul Zweig

The Night is Our Dress

The night, the holy water, flows inside us
The holy night the holy water
Rises calmly and slowly lifts us up
The night, the third body inside us
Its heart is of diamond and that is why
We shine within, my beloved

The night is our dress, it strips us bare;
Its fur is black and white
Beast from the inner jungle, drinking our blood
Not the black or the red blood, but the white.
O how naked we are, my loved one, in this net of stars!
And our double angel shines its phosphorescent rays.

—Translated from the French by Paul Zweig

Elegy for Poor Me

What did you do with the fireproof angel
You were to have kept in the tower of flesh?
Perhaps it was too narrow for him
In this body which fifty pains
Have built between mildewed walls
And the fiery angel bruised
His singing wings on its bars?

I don't love you any more, my poor ego,
So busy with your dust
Always cleaning the screws of your skeleton
Rubbing the rust off your knees
Wiping the oxide from your green temples

I don't love you any more, stranger
Who sleeps when the storks of joy
Fly in their vees toward a fable
When the bee-swarm crowns the evening's ecstasy
I don't love you any more, for you
No longer remember the delights of the angels

A taste of chalk has been on my tongue
Since the purple wing caught fire
Since the hand of friendship
Dried up like the hand of an elm in October
Revealing the veins without love

I am alone I am alone in the tower of my flesh
I open my voiceless mouth
And I close my sightless eye
I am alone I am alone
Because the angel has abandoned me

Sometimes hunger drives me out of my prison
I go to meet those who weigh the time
Those who sell the golden fish
Those who laugh while they nail up coffins
And those in the Babylon of ants
Whom it bores to dream in freedom

At the foot of the olive trees the brooks cascade
Through the white cliffs
So too my blood cascades
Between the ruin of my shoulderblades

One day when the rocks no longer change into sand
When the ocean retreats from my heart
The fiery-haired angel will return
To deal out justice

—Translated from the German by George Hitchcock

Marcel *MIHALOVICI*
Portrait d'Yvan GOLL.
Encre de chine - 1939. (OA 12)

APPENDIX

1-"Manifeste du surréalisme," *Surréalisme*, I, Paris: October 1924, pp. [viii - ix].

Surréalisme. Paris:Éditions Jean-Michel Place, 2004. A facsimile edition of Goll's 1924 edition of *Surréalisme* with commentary, "Autour de la revue Surréalisme," by Jean Bertho.

Sources: Jeremy Stubbs, "Goll versus Breton: The Battle for Surrealism," in *Yvan Goll—Claire Goll: Texts and Contexts*, ed. Eric Roberson and Robert Vilain. Amsterdam-Atlanta: Rodopi, 1997.

Gérard Durozoi: *History of the Surrealist Movement*, trans. Alison Anderon. Chicago: University of Chicago Press, 2002. Translated from the French by Nan Watkins with Gerlinde M. Lindy, *Asheville Poetry Review.*

2- First published as a booklet, *Der Panama-Kanal*, under the pseudonym Iwan Lassang. Berlin-Wilmersdorf: A.R. Meyer, 1914. Translation from: Yvan Goll: Die Lyrik in vier Bänden. Band I. Frühe Gedichte. 1906-1930, hg. u. kommentiert v. Barbara Glauert-Hesse im Auftrag der Fondation Yvan et Claire Goll, Saint-Dié-des-Vosges. © Argon Verlag, Berlin 1996. All rights retained and reserved by Wallstein Verlag, Göttingen. Translated from the German by Nan Watkins, *House Organ*, 2014.

3- *Jean Sans Terre* (1936-1939)—American Edition: Thomas Yoseloff Publisher, 1958 — (misc. translators from the French).

4- *Fruit From Saturn*, 1946—Hemispheres Press, (composed in English by Yvan Goll)
"Atom Elegy" sections II, III, IV.

5- *Le Mythe de la Roche Percée*, 1947— translated from the French by Frank Jones, Mill Mountain Press, 1975.

6- *Elégie de Lackawanner*, 1947—Sumac Press Edition, 1970, (translated from the French by Galway Kinnell).

7- *Dix Mille Aubes,* 1951-—White Pine Press, Buffalo, NY, 2004 (translated from the French by Thomas Rain Crowe).

8- *Traumkraut,* Limes Verlag, 1951 — Black Lawrence Press, 2012 (translated from the German by Nan Watkins).

9- *Yvan Goll: Selected Poems,* 1968 — Edited by Paul Zweig, Kayak Books Inc. (Miscellaneous translators, translated from the French).

Yvan GOLL au Jardin Zoologique - New York, 1944. (H.C.)

ABOUT THE EDITOR

Thomas Rain Crowe   is an internationally-published and recognized author and translator of more than thirty books, including the multi-award winning nonfiction nature memoir *Zoro's Field: My Life in the Appalachian Woods* (2005); an historical novel *The Watcher: Like Sweet Bells Jangled* (2015); an anthology of contemporary Celtic language poets from six European countries titled *Writing the Wind: A Celtic Resurgence (The New Celtic Poetry)*, 1997; several collections of poems including *Radiogenesis* (2007) and *The Laugharne Poems* published in Wales in 1997 by Carreg Gwalch, and most recently a literary memoir *Starting From San Francisco: The Baby Beat Generation and the 2nd San Francisco Renaissance* published by Third Mind Books in 2018. He is the translator along with Nan Watkins of *10,000 Dawns: The Love Poems of Yvan and Claire Goll* published by White Pine Press in 2004. He has been an editor of major literary and cultural journals and anthologies and   is founder and publisher of New Native Press (www.newnativepress.org).   He is a longtime resident of the Southern Appalachians and lives in the Tuckasegee watershed and the "Little Canada" community of Jackson County in western North Carolina.